What's in this book

This book belongs to

____

动物真奇妙 Amazing animals

学习内容 Contents

沟通 Communication

说说动物名称
Say the names of animals

描述动物外貌
Describe animal's physical appearance

生词 New words

★	去	to go to
★	老虎	tiger
★	狮子	lion
★	只	(measure word for certain animals)
★	马	horse
★	羊	sheep
★	熊	bear
★	熊猫	panda
	动物	animal
	动物园	zoo

长颈鹿	giraffe
猴子	monkey
蛇	snake
短	short

文化 Cultures

中国的珍稀动物——熊猫

Panda — A vulnerable animal in China

句式 Sentence patterns

蛇的身体长。

The body of the snake is long.

这只熊的尾巴短短的。

This bear has a short tail.

跨学科学习 Project

了解动物的食物来源

Learn about how animals find their food

Get ready

1. Do you like going to the zoo?
2. What is your favourite animal?
3. What animals can you see here?

你喜欢动物吗？
喜欢去动物园吗？

老虎和狮子，它们的眼睛和鼻子很相像。

马比这只羊高，比那只长颈鹿矮。

蛇的身体长，猴子的尾
巴也长。

熊的尾巴短短的，熊猫的眼睛黑黑的。

快去动物园看看我们奇妙的朋友吧！

Let's think

1 Circle the parts which do not belong with the animals.

2 How many legs do they have? Draw some animals in each group and say.

New words

02 **1** Learn the new words.

去

只

老虎　狮子　马　羊　动物园

短

熊　熊猫　长颈鹿　猴子　蛇

2 Which sentence is correct? Put a tick or a cross.

这只羊比马高。

老虎和狮子在一起。

这不是熊猫。
这是熊。

听听说说 Listen and say

03 **1** Listen and number the pictures.

04 **2** Look at the pictures. Listen to the sto

d say.

3 Write the letters and role-play.

a 长长的　b 去
c 短短的　d 只

我是蛇。我的
身体 ___。

我是一 ___ 熊。
我有 ___ 尾巴。

我是老虎。
我喜欢 ___
那里喝水。

Task

How do the animals move? Match and describe the animals.

这是一只熊。熊有短短的尾巴，黑色的鼻子，圆圆的肚子。

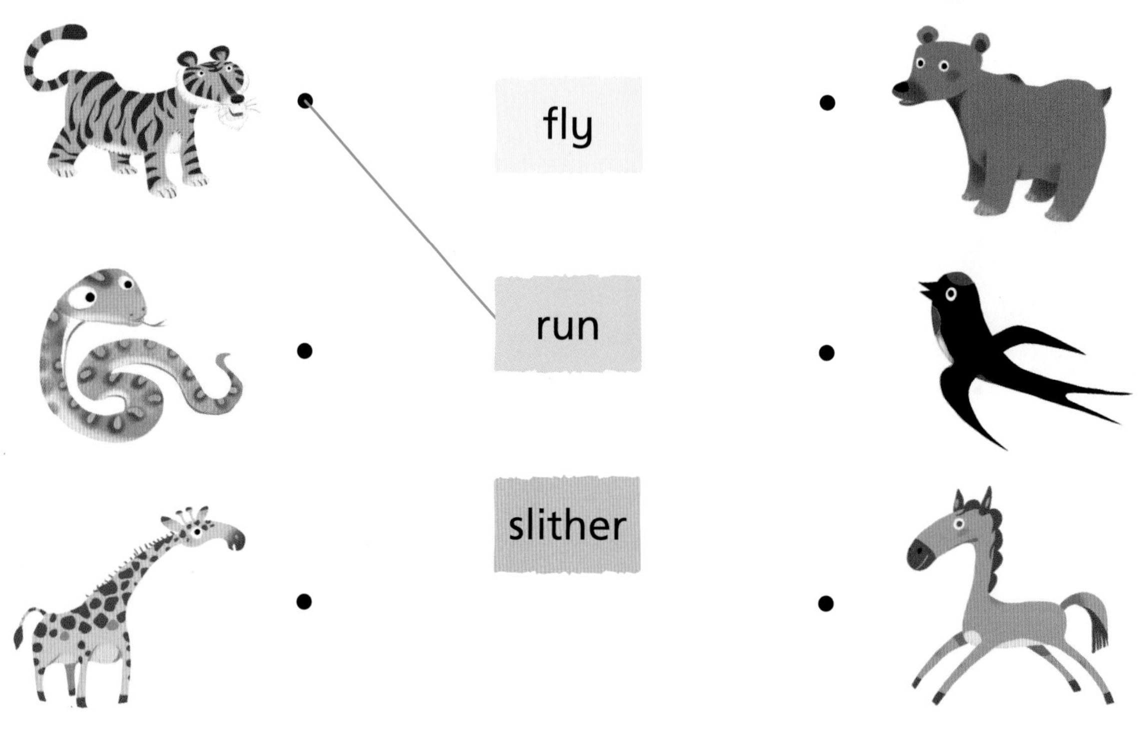

Game

Make and paint an animal mask. Talk with your friend.

我是老虎。
我好看吗？

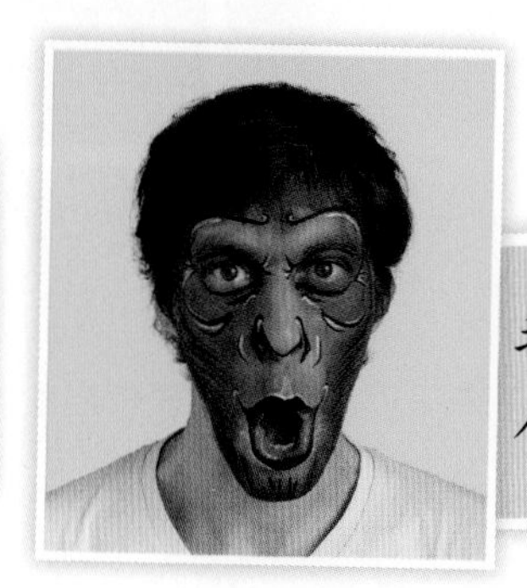

我是猴子。我的尾巴长长的。
你是什么动物？

Song

Listen and sing.

动物园

我去动物园，我去动物园，
看老虎和狮子。
还有熊和马，
羊和猴子，
真好看！真好看！

我不知道。
I don't know.

我不明白。
I don't understand.

写一写 Write

1 Learn and trace the strokes.

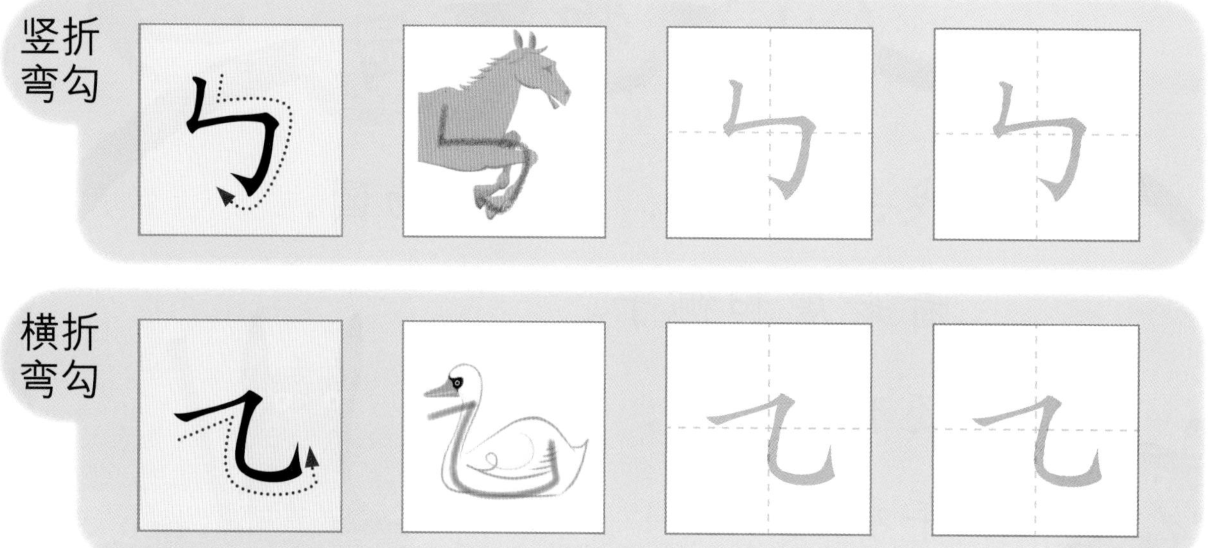

2 Learn the component. Colour 马 in the characters.

3 Colour ㄣ red and ㄟ blue.

4 Trace and write the characters.

5 Write and say.

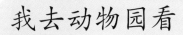

我去动物园看

老  和  。

汉字小常识 Did you know?

Some characters include a component that encloses another component on three sides — left, top and right.

Colour the component that encloses another component blue.

Cultures

1 Pandas are adored by the world. Have you seen one before?

Pandas, or giant pandas, have unique black-and-white marks and live in south central China. They mostly eat bamboo and are one of the vulnerable species in the world.

我喜欢吃竹子！

2 How many pandas are there living in the world now? Research and report.

现在有 ________ 只大熊猫。大熊猫有黑色的眼睛和耳朵，白色的身体。

Project

1 Do you know how animals obtain their food? Research and finish the chart.

a 猴子 b 马 c 老虎 d 长颈鹿 e 蛇

Some animals obtain their food from plants and some from other animals. There are also animals which eat both animals and plants for food.

2 Colour the right paths red for the monkey to find its food.

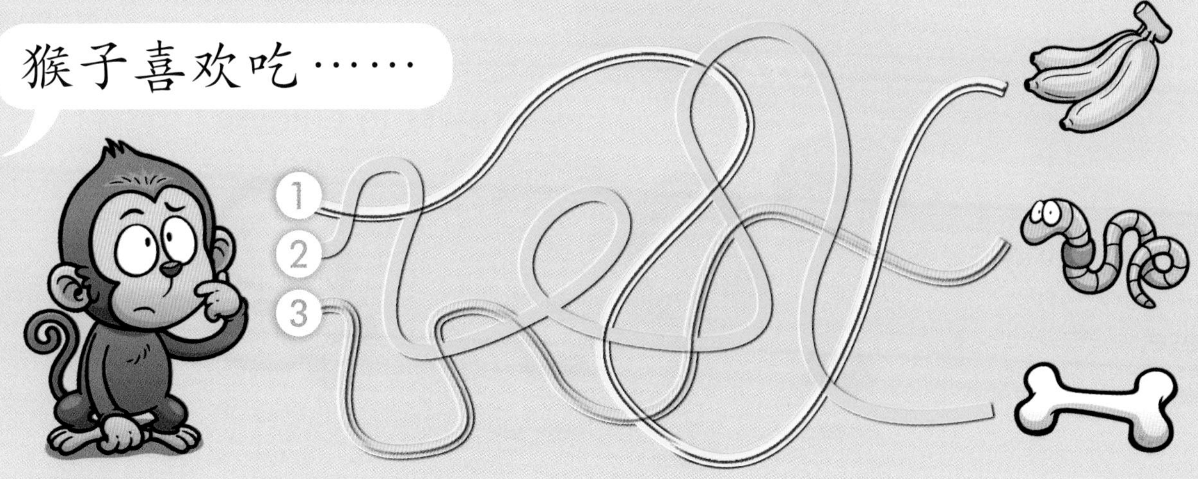

1 Find the starting point in the board game and play.

Say 'The giraffe is taller than the sheep.' in Chinese.

Write the character.

老

这是什么动物？
Answer in Chinese.

熊的耳朵短短的。

这里有一只狮子。

START

Say 'I like going to the zoo.' in Chinese.

这是什么动物？
Answer in Chinese.

Write the character.

2 Work with your friend. Colour the stars and the chillies.

Words	说	读	写
去	☆	☆	🌶
老虎	☆	☆	🌶
狮子	☆	☆	🌶
只	☆	☆	🌶
马	☆	☆	☆
羊	☆	☆	🌶
熊	☆	☆	🌶
熊猫	☆	☆	🌶
动物	☆	🌶	🌶
动物园	☆	🌶	🌶
长颈鹿	☆	🌶	🌶

Words and sentences	说	读	写
猴子	☆	🌶	🌶
蛇	☆	🌶	🌶
短	☆	🌶	🌶
蛇的身体长。	☆	🌶	🌶
这只熊的尾巴短短的。	☆	🌶	🌶

Say the names of animals	☆
Describe animal's physical appearance	☆

3 What does your teacher say?

My teacher says ...

分享 Sharing

Words I remember

去	qù	to go to
老虎	lǎo hǔ	tiger
狮子	shī zi	lion
只	zhī	(measure word for certain animals)
马	mǎ	horse
羊	yáng	sheep
熊	xióng	bear
熊猫	xióng māo	panda
动物	dòng wù	animal
动物园	dòng wù yuán	zoo

长颈鹿	cháng jǐng lù	giraffe
猴子	hóu zi	monkey
蛇	shé	snake
短	duǎn	short

Other words

它们	tā men	they, them
很	hěn	very
相像	xiāng xiàng	similar
尾巴	wěi bā	tail
快	kuài	quickly
奇妙	qí miào	amazing
竹子	zhú zi	bamboo

OXFORD
UNIVERSITY PRESS

Oxford University Press is a department of the University of Oxford.
It furthers the University's objective of excellence in research, scholarship,
and education by publishing worldwide. Oxford is a registered trade mark of
Oxford University Press in the UK and in certain other countries

Published in Hong Kong by
Oxford University Press (China) Limited
39th Floor, One Kowloon, 1 Wang Yuen Street, Kowloon Bay,
Hong Kong

First Edition published in 2017

Illustrated by Anne Lee and Wildman

Photographs for reproduction permitted by Dreamstime.com

China National Publications Import & Export (Group) Corporation is an authorized distributor of Oxford Elementary Chinese.

Please contact content@cnpiec.com.cn or 86-10-65856782

ISBN: 978-0-19-082199-9

10 9 8 7 6 5 4 3 2